Care About Quality

Your Guide to Child Care

Child Development Division
California Department of Education

800-KIDS-793

Publishing Information

Care About Quality was developed by the California Department of Education, Child Development Division, and was published by the Department, 721 Capitol Mall, Sacramento, California (mailing address: P.O. Box 944272, Sacramento, CA 94244-2720). It was distributed under the provisions of the Library Distribution Act and *Government Code* Section 11096.

Project Coordinators: Alice Trathen and Kari Hazen
Design: Sugarman Design and Laurel Mathe
Photography: Roy Wilcox Photography
Layout: Hazen Publishing, Inc.

ISBN 0-8011-1497-7

Ordering Information

Limited copies of this publication are available from the California Department of Education. Please send a written request to the California Department of Education, Child Development Division, Alice Trathen, 560 J. St., Room 220, Sacramento, CA 95814; FAX (916) 323-8054.

In addition, an illustrated *Educational Resources Catalog* describing publications, videos, and other instructional media available from the Department can be obtained without charge by writing to CDE Press, Sales Office, P.O. Box 271, Sacramento, CA 95812-0271 or by calling the Sales Office at (916) 445-1260.

Notice

The guidance in *Care About Quality* is not binding on local educational agencies or other entities. Except for the statutes, regulations, and court decisions that are referenced herein, the document is exemplary, and compliance with it is not mandatory. (See Education Code Section 33308.5.)

Every effort has been made to trace the ownership of all copyrighted material included in this volume. Any errors that may have occurred are inadvertent and will be corrected in subsequent editions, provided notification is sent to the publisher.

8 0 0 - K I D S - 7 9 3

Care About Quality

Table of Contents

Acknowledgments

The development of this guide is the result of the input from many knowledgeable individuals and organizations serving California's children in early care and education. Their insight brought meaning to its purpose by offering information that is simple to understand and enjoyable to read.

Many thanks to California Child Care Resource and Referral Network representatives, Child Action of Sacramento, National Association for the Education of Young Children (NAEYC), Parent Voices, Children's Council of San Francisco, Central Valley Children's Services Network, Family Resources and Referral Center serving San Joaquin County, San Juan Unified School District's Dewey Discovery Club, and the Auburn Discovery Montessori School.

Many thanks to Sharon Hawley, Barbara Metzuk, Malia Ramler, Center for Health Training, Family Child Care Association, Rosemary Couverette, Pamm Shaw, Laura Bridges, Joan Richards, Linda Nissen, Kelley Knapp, Dianne Cromwell, Pat Spahr, Joanne Hahn, Terri Foust, Nadine Roberts, Arlene Evans, Judith Kinter, Elizabeth Gillogoy, Georgia Hughes, Gayle Kelly, and the others who contributed to this guide. A special thank you to CDE Press representatives, the staff of Deen & Black Public Relations, and Kari Hazen.

Alice Trathen

Alice Trathen,
Child Development Consultant
Project Leader

Introduction

Whether you work full time or part time or just need an occasional caregiver, quality child care is a necessity for both you and your child. While no one can replace a loving parent, an excellent child care provider can enrich your child's life and give you peace of mind that your child is in good hands.

For some, choosing quality child care is simple—a favorite family member offers to care for your child. For others, the search turns into a series of phone calls, questions, and visits to child care providers. In other words, you may spend a great deal of time searching for the right caregiver.

Trust should be a primary issue when choosing child care. Trust begins at the first interview and continues throughout your entire child care experience. Having confidence in your provider is one of the ways you know you've found quality child care. The bottom line is, you need to feel that the child care arrangement you select will be a safe and loving experience in which your child will thrive.

This resource guide is provided by the California Department of Education to help you find quality child care. I hope that the tips, checklists, and vital information it includes will help you ask the right questions, locate the right resources, and ultimately, find the best possible care for your child.

If I have my way, California will one day have the highest quality child development programs universally available. We have many good programs, and we hope to have many more in our great state. In the meantime, we hope you find this guide useful.

Delaine Eastin

Delaine Eastin
State Superintendent of Public Instruction

Defining quality child care

While no one can replace you, quality child care will offer your child a stimulating, nurturing environment which should help prepare him for school and to reach his full potential.

So what exactly is quality child care? Well, quality is defined as a degree of excellence. This means not average, not "it will do" child care, but excellent child care. Bottom line, you need to feel that the child care provider you select will offer a safe and stimulating, loving environment in which your child will mentally and physically thrive.

Characteristics of quality

As you begin your search, here's what to look for in quality child care:

- Settings that are safe and provide small group sizes and adult-to-child ratios encouraging the best opportunities for development;
- Caregivers or teachers who have experience and are trained in early childhood development;
- Settings that offer opportunities for meaningful parent involvement;

1

- Learning materials and teaching styles that are age-appropriate and respectful of children's cultural and ethnic heritage; and
- Learning opportunities that promote your child's success in school.

(Adapted from "What are the benefits of high quality?" National Association for the Education of Young Children, 1509 16th Street NW, Washington, D.C. 20036-1426)

It's never too early to start your child care search

One thing is certain: you can never begin your child care search too soon. If possible, start your child care search at least six months before you need the care. The more time and thought you put into choosing your provider, the better you'll feel with your choice. One of the best places to find help is your local resource and referral agency.

Choosing quality child care

While the many choices and varying advice regarding child care may seem overwhelming, in the end your feelings will help you choose your provider.

Your local child care resource and referral (R&R) agency offers a wealth of information right at your fingertips—and it's free. Child care resource and referral agencies are located in every county in California. Take a look at what resource and referral agencies offer.

They:

- Provide parents, organizations, and leaders with information about child care and assist in planning for future child care needs.
- Maintain the most up-to-date and accurate list of child care providers in your community, including licensed family child care homes and child care centers.
- Track child care providers' licensing status, the languages the providers speak, the age groups of children they serve, the schedules they offer, and the number of spaces available in family child care homes or centers.
- Work with providers to improve the quality of child care and to maintain and expand the number of child care providers needed in your county.
- Provide training and other services that help providers stay in business.

3

- Teach parents, organizations, and leaders about child care and how to plan for future child care issues and needs.

Your local child care resource and referral agency is just a call away. By dialing 1-800-KIDS-793, you can get the phone number of your county's resource and referral agency. Your local R&R will help you take the first steps in finding quality child care.

Taking the first steps in your decision

- Write down what you want from your child care provider. Think about what your child may also want. Ask her, if she is old enough.
- Talk to the staff at your local resource and referral agency, read parenting publications, and ask trusted friends and co-workers for references on child care providers and programs.
- Think about what you can afford. Check into any child care financial assistance through the State or your employer. What will your monthly budget allow?
- Interview caregivers on the phone. Ask about staff-to-child ratios, costs, the learning opportunities offered, and whether the provider is licensed. Use the checklists in this guide to help you make

your choice. Remember, there may be times in the day when a child care provider is unable to speak with you because she is caring for children. You may be asked to call back at a certain time or to stop by and visit.

The visit

A visit provides more information than any phone conversation. Make sure you visit while the provider is offering child care. Look around the child care facility or home:

- What is your first impression? Are the children smiling, active, and nurtured?
- Is this a place where you want your child to spend his waking and sleeping hours? Will your child like being here? Would your child feel safe?
- Would your child find the indoor and outdoor space of this home or center a fun place to play, learn, and explore?
- How many caregivers and children are there?
- Is the provider licensed, and if so, how many children is she licensed for?
- Are parents encouraged to visit at any time and without notice?
- Does the provider have a business contract or something in writing that explains how the provider operates? Are fees, vacations, sick days, and hours of operation included in the agreement?

Parent Tip

One of the best sources in finding quality child care is through the resource and referral (R&R) agencies. These agencies provide child care referrals and a variety of information to all parents as well as the community about the availability of child care within all counties in California. The R&Rs also assist potential providers in the licensing process, offer information about training for caregivers, and promote quality services in early care and education programs.

5

- What happens if the provider is no longer able to offer care? Does the provider have a "back-up" caregiver in case she is ill?
- Are the equipment and toys safe and materials age-appropriate?
- Is there a comfortable and quiet place for children to play or relax away from others?
- Are there activities that will interest your child and keep her busy?
- Does the child care setting seem organized? Are there cubbies or color-coded crates with a variety of toys and art materials?
- Does the provider share information with you regarding your child's progress?
- Is the child care setting rich with books, letters and numbers, paper, and other supplies?
- Are the provider's values consistent with your own?
- When and how is television used?
- Is parent input and involvement encouraged?
- How are birthdays or special occasions celebrated? Do the celebrations include your child's and others cultural backgrounds?

Depending on the age of your child, there are several types of child care you may need to consider. The following provides a description of settings from infant to school-age child care.

Infant and toddler care

When looking for quality care for infants and toddlers, look for a provider who seems to enjoy your child by talking and interacting with her in a warm, friendly way. It is important that your little one is included in activities but stays safe when around older children. Keep these questions in mind when looking for quality infant and toddler care:

- Does the provider keep a clean diaper changing area which can be disinfected after every diaper change?
- Does she wash her hands after every diaper change and between diaper changes?
- What are the sleeping arrangements? Where are cribs located?
- What experience has the provider had with infants and toddlers?
- Who supplies the diapers? Formula? Baby food?
- How is your infant fed? Is she held and cuddled with every bottle feeding? Fed on her own schedule?
- Does the provider encourage you to bring breast milk and stop in throughout the day to breast-feed your baby?
- Is there a special outside play area for infants and toddlers?
- What are the ages of the other children?
- What is the provider's plan for dealing with separation and attachment issues which happen during the first years of life?
- Does the provider ask you what your child likes and needs?
- Does the provider read, sing, and provide toys that are appropriate for your child's age?

Preschool care

Preschoolers need room to run, jump, climb, and socialize. Look for a provider that can expose your child to books, toys, art, music, and "share time," which will help him prepare for school without pushing him too much.

Find out:

- What is the preschool's daily schedule?
- Do the providers interact with the children and stay close to observe them?
- Do the providers get down to the level of the child? Is eye contact being made?
- Do the children respond in a positive way to the providers?
- Do you see smiles exchanged?
- With regard to art projects, does the provider believe that process or product is the more important?
- Are there creative materials for pretending so that the children can use their imagination at all times?
- How much climbing, running, or jumping will the children have each day?
- Is correct language used?
- When are books used? Is there a regular story time?
- Is there a balance between active and quiet play?
- Is there child-sized equipment?

- Are toys stored within easy reach of the children, or must they always ask an adult?
- How is toilet training handled?
- Are children required to take a nap?
- Are children encouraged to help with cleanup?

School-age care

Quality school-age care offers a safe, friendly, and stimulating environment for older children when they are not in school. Children need to be supervised at all times. Indoor and outdoor activities should be stimulating and fun for this age group. School-age care also needs to be flexible to offer a program that meets the individual needs of children. Here are some questions to consider when looking for quality school-age care:

- Is transportation provided to and from school? If necessary, is the provider on the bus route?
- Are afternoon snacks available?
- What about homework? Is there access to a quiet study place, computers or other learning tools?

9

- Does the program provide tutoring for children who need extra help?
- Does the provider feel comfortable with visits from school friends on site? Is there transportation for after-school activities, such as sports, piano, Little League, or 4-H?
- Is the method of discipline appropriate for older children? Do the children have some say in organizing their day?

Other points to consider

Whether you are looking for infant, preschool, or school-age care, read the caregiver's written policies and procedures. Determine when the program is closed and what the policy is for late pickup or illness. Check references. Talk with other parents who have children in the program. When you have narrowed down your choices, contact two important agencies that will help check on the past history of providers: your local Community Care Licensing and/or TrustLine. Visit the program at least twice, at different times of the day. Stay long enough to watch children switch from one activity to another.

Making your choice

Before making your final choice, bring your child to visit the child care provider(s) or center. Watch:

- How does your child get along with the provider(s)? The other children? Is she excited about being cared for there?
- How does your child interact with the other children?
- Does your child seem comfortable with the meals provided?
- How does the daily schedule work for your child?
- What is the next step in starting the child care relationship?
- Is there a waiting list?

Talk to the provider again and ask for written fee information. If possible, enroll your child in the child care program a few days before returning to work to ensure a smooth transition.

Child care centers

No two child care facilities are exactly alike. From a large child care center to a neighbor's home to care in your own living room—many choices are open to parents seeking quality child care. Knowing the types of child care available and how they can best meet the needs of both you and your child are the first steps in making the right choice.

Child care centers are required to be licensed in California. Infants, toddlers, preschool, or school-age children may all receive care at a child care center. Centers are usually located in schools, religious facilities, public buildings, or private buildings. A center may be a part of a large child care corporation or it may be locally owned. Some centers focus on a specific teaching method, such as High Scope, Montessori, or Waldorf. Center programs tend to be organized around the care and education of a larger group of children.

Separate licenses are required to care for infants, preschoolers, and school-age children, although a center may be licensed to care for all three age groups at one site. Depending on their age, children receive care in separate areas at the center for safety and activity reasons.

Centers are located in schools, religious facilities, public buildings, or private buildings.

11

Ratios

The staffing ratios for child care programs are established by the State of California to provide minimum standards for adult supervision at a child care center. Ratios of caregivers to children vary depending on the age of the child and the number of trained staff members present. When looking at a child care center ask:

- How many trained staff members care for infants and preschoolers?
- Find out the number of trained staff that supervise school-age children.
- Contact your local resource and referral agency and licensing office to double-check the staff-to-child ratio. Call 1-800-KIDS-793 for the agencies in your area.

Parent Tip

Staffing ratios, or the number of staff per child, are a very important factor to consider when choosing quality child care. A ratio establishes a minimum standard a provider must follow to receive and retain a child care license. There are also many types of child care licenses, and the ratios are different depending upon the age of the children and the number of adults. Make sure you feel comfortable with the number of children being cared for by the provider. For more information about ratios, contact the Community Care Licensing Office at (916) 229-4269 for help.

Staff qualifications

Qualified teachers for centers that care for infants or preschoolers must have completed at least twelve units of early childhood education. For teachers in centers with a license for school-age children, the units may be in multiple education subjects or recreation-related fields appropriate for the care of older children. Additionally, employees of centers may be a part of several professional organizations and/or may attend continuing professional education courses.

Points to consider in choosing a child care center

- **Environment:** How many caregivers will be with your child in a day or week? Are there plenty of interesting toys and materials for your child to play with? Is the center organized so your child can find things easily? Are the children smiling and happy?

- **Values:** What are the provider's philosophy and values? How does the provider discipline children? How does the provider individualize learning activities, nap, mealtime, and toilet training?

- **Communication:** How does the center staff share information about your child's progress and daily activities? Can you visit at any time? How is discipline handled?

- **Staff:** How long have the caregivers worked at the center? What is the staff turnover? Are the management's and caregivers' values the same? Does the staff seem relaxed and responsive to the children's needs?

- **Parent Involvement:** Are you welcome to participate in the child care program? Are you required to volunteer? Does staff encourage your input on how well your child is doing? How is your child's progress shared with you?

- **Education:** What type of experience, education, and credentials do the caregivers have? Is the center a member of the NAEYC?

- **Licensing:** What type of license does the center have? Can your child attend from infancy to school-age? Did you contact Community Care Licensing to check on any previous complaints?

- **Location:** How convenient is it for you from your work, home, bus route, and/or health care provider?

- **Cost:** Can you afford the monthly tuition? Is there an additional registration fee? Is there a family discount? Does the center charge a fee for late pickup? Are there any other costs for materials, field trips, or books?

- **Evaluation:** Does the program staff have a process of determining what they are doing well and what needs to be worked on?

Family child care homes

Licensed family child care homes refer to child care in an individual's private home. The home may be rented, leased, or owned. It may be in a mobile home park or in an apartment. Because family child care is home-based, children tend to be cared for in a family-like setting with all the daily activities usually associated with home. The types of family child care homes vary widely, from the neighborhood parent who cares for a few children to a large family child care home that cares for up to 14 children. A family child care home is a business. You should expect professional service and should treat your provider as a professional.

Ratios

The number of children cared for at a family child care home may vary, depending on the age of the children and whether an assistant is present. The children of the provider and assistant who are under the age of ten are included in determining the adult-to-child ratio. When looking at a family child care home:

- Find out how many adults and children are present.
- Ask the provider the number of children she is licensed for.

The types of family child care homes vary widely, from the neighborhood parent who cares for a few children to a large family child care home that cares for up to 14 children.

- Ask if she cares for school-age children.
- Finally, when you contact your local resource and referral agency and Community Care Licensing, double-check the ratio.

Staff qualifications

Family child care providers are required to be licensed if they care for the children of more than one family. Licensing has minimum health and safety standards that providers must follow. Licensing requires that providers take pediatric CPR, first aid, and health and safety classes. Providers may have additional education, such as a degree in early childhood education, community college courses, or training through child care associations. Providers may receive accreditation through the National Association for Family Child Care (NAFCC). This organization's mission is to recognize high quality in family child care.

Toys increase children's social and emotional development and improve their gross and fine motor coordination. Here are some guidelines to help you choose safe toys for your child. Ask:

- *What is the manufacturer's recommended age for the toy?*
- *Is it nontoxic?*
- *Is it washable?*
- *If it's electrical, does it carry the "UL Approved" label?*
- *Is it BIG enough to prevent choking?*
- *Is it sturdy with smooth edges and no small or loose parts?*
- *Does it have strings or cords that wrap around a child's neck?*
- *And finally, never let a child under five play with a balloon.*

15

Points to consider in choosing family child care

- **Environment:** Is the home clean and safe? Are latches on cabinets, plugs on outlets? Are the stairs, fireplace, and windows child-proofed? Are there any physical concerns you may have, such as a pool or unused cars or equipment in the backyard? Does the provider keep firearms in the home? If so, are they locked up and stored away from reach? Are there plenty of interesting and age-appropriate toys and materials for your child to play with? Does the provider offer a preschool program or help prepare your child for school? Does the provider offer transportation to and from school? If the provider transports your children, is the provider trained on car seat and vehicle safety? Ask about the provider's driving record.
- **Values:** What are the provider's philosophy and values? How does the provider discipline children? How does the provider individualize learning activities, nap, mealtime, and toilet training?
- **Communication:** Does the caregiver share information with you on how your child is doing? Can you visit at any time?
- **Experience:** How long has the caregiver provided child care? What type of education does she have? Did you contact Community Care Licensing for the caregiver's past history?
- **Operation:** What hours does it operate? Does this provider offer evening, early morning, or weekend hours? What age and how many children will the provider care for? What is the staff-to-child care ratio the home must follow? Does the caregiver have children at home? Are the children counted in the ratio?
- **Location:** Where is the home? Is it close to your work, home, and health care provider?
- **Cost:** What are the monthly fees? Late fees? Registration fees? Is there a vacation or sick leave credit when your child is out?
- **Back-up plan:** What is the provider's back-up plan? When does the provider go on vacation or take personal holidays? What types of experience do the assistant or substitute caregivers have?

In-home care

There are several options if you prefer to have your child cared for in your home. The most common choice is care for your child by another family member in your home. In-home care is legally called license-exempt, which means that a child care license is not needed to care for your child. In-home care is convenient as everything you need for your child is right under your own roof. In-home providers either come to your home for certain hours or live in your home. They care for your child and may help with daily home chores such as laundry and meals. Be clear about what is expected. Talk to your provider about what your child did during the day and watch your child's behavior. Here are types of in-home choices:

Relative care

This is care provided by any relative in their home or your home. Any number of children may be cared for as long as they are all related. A license is not required. Make sure you talk to your relative openly and honestly. Talk about money. Is there any to be exchanged? What about feelings and past history with each other? Most important, talk about your child and what he needs to be well cared for. Thank your relative, as you would any provider, often and let her know you appreciate the care.

The most common choice is care for your child by another family member in your home. In-home care is legally called license-exempt, which means that a child care license is not needed to care for your child.

17

Nannies

Nannies may be found through local agencies, which may screen and interview candidates and usually link you with a provider. Nanny agencies are required to use the TrustLine background check when placing a provider. Nannies may also be found through a faith-based organization, a friend, or an ad in the paper. Annual salaries for a full-time nanny hired through an agency can range from $10,000 to $22,000 or more. Parents may also pay an agency fee for placement. Before hiring a nanny, you should talk with an accountant or bookkeeper familiar with household employee laws. The IRS can provide you with the forms needed to employ an in-home provider. On top of federal taxes, you are also responsible for state taxes.

Au pair

An au pair is usually a foreign student who exchanges child care services for living arrangements and a small salary. The arrangement usually covers a maximum of one year. Au pairs are able to perform child care and light housekeeping duties related to child care for approximately 45 hours a week. The nation's au pair organizations are licensed by the U.S. Information Agency in Washington, D.C. Au pair pay is mandated by this agency, and

Parent Tip

When a family member or friend watches your child or children, make sure you talk about how the child care arrangement will work before actually committing to it. Talk about money, hours, what your child needs, discipline, and how you will handle any disagreements. Be sensitive to the family relationship and make sure you do not take advantage of it.

800-KIDS-793

fees may be as much as $150 a week. Other costs for an au pair include full room and board, an educational payment of $500, additional insurance if your au pair uses the family car, and other minimal costs.

Hiring tips

While nanny and au pair agencies may screen candidates, there are no licensing standards that candidates must meet.

Points to consider in choosing in-home care

- **Background:** What is the provider's background? What is her experience caring for children? Did you contact TrustLine at 1-800-822-8490?
- **Screening:** What type of background screening was done on the individual? Did you check references? Were fingerprints checked? Was the individual registered with TrustLine? Is the provider CPR and first aid certified?
- **Responsibilities:** Do you have a written job description to give to the candidate? Do you understand the financial and legal responsibilities of in-home care? What is your back-up plan in case the provider is sick or on vacation? What other options do you have if the in-home situation does not work?

TrustLine offers parents the chance to evaluate a child care provider. It is a registry of in-home child care providers who have cleared a background screening through a fingerprint check of records at the California Department of Justice. This means they have no disqualifying criminal convictions or substantiated child abuse reports in California.
To contact Trustline, call 1-800-822-8490 or visit the Internet at www.trustline.org.

Child care for your child with special needs

All children have special needs. However, some children, because of physical, emotional, or learning needs, may require extra support in the child care setting. It is very important to choose child care that meets your basic requirements first—then address your child's unique needs with the provider.

Things to consider

- If a child care provider has never cared for a child with special needs, he may be fearful or uncomfortable until he gets to know your child. You are the most knowledgeable person about your child's needs, so it is important for you to share with the provider information and ideas that you have found work best.
- Children often act differently in the child care setting than at home, so don't be surprised if your suggestions don't always work out.
- Caring for a child with special needs is a partnership among the family, child care providers, and any specialists involved.

It is the right of every child to have high-quality, safe, and nurturing child care. It is your responsibility to choose the best care for your child and help providers know that they CAN meet the special needs of your child—and that you'll help them do it.

- The Americans with Disabilities Act (ADA) requires child care programs to make "reasonable" efforts to accommodate a child with a disability.

There are other resources that can help you. Family resource centers provide parent-to-parent support and training. Regional centers link families of children ages birth to three years who have or are at risk of developmental disabilities to early intervention programs in each county. You can call **1-800-515-BABY** to get the number of your local family resource center or regional center.

Children ages birth to three who qualify for early intervention services receive an **individualized family service plan (IFSP)**. The IFSP identifies the special services and who will provide them. Once your child turns three, if he is eligible for special services, such as speech therapy, they are provided by the school district through an **individualized education program (IEP)**. These plans describe the goals for your child and the services to help meet them.

Finding child care

Some child care resource and referral agencies match families with caregivers who specialize in working with children with special needs. Call the child care provider and ask about policies, fees, schedules, and activities to determine if this setting is a good fit for your child before discussing the disability. AFTER you feel comfortable with a provider, let her know about your child's special needs in a way that is nonthreatening and supportive. This lets the child care provider know that you are concerned with her skill and ability to help your child and you will provide her with the necessary resources, training, and support to care to care for your child's special needs.

If you feel that a child care program is discriminating against your child because of her disability, you can get legal advice from the Child Care Law Center at 415-495-5498.

Choosing special needs care

When choosing child care for a child with special needs:

1. Interview caregivers as you would for any child.
2. Ask for references and check them out.
3. Visit *without* your child first. Make sure you are comfortable with the type of care provided.
4. *Then* bring your child to the child care setting and observe how she reacts or adjusts to the staff, the materials, and the other children.
5. When you are ready, start your child's care for an hour or so, gradually increasing the time until he gets used to the provider and the provider is secure in meeting his needs.

Children with special needs require different levels of support and care. The willingness and openness of the provider to work with specialists in coordination and partnership with the family is crucial in providing high-quality child care for your child.

In your search for quality child care, the following checklists may be helpful:

Caregiver considerations

- Has special training, skills, or experience with children with special needs.
- Works as a team member with family and specialists.
- Communicates regularly about the child's development and any concerns as they arise.
- Maintains confidentiality and with your permission answers questions regarding the child's special needs.
- Has a system to record medication, special feedings, or other procedures.

Environmental considerations

- Facility is accessible and safe for the child, accommodates adaptive equipment (e.g., wheelchairs, walkers).
- Toys and play materials are within the child's reach.
- There are enough adults present to meet children's individual needs.
- The overall group size is not too large to be overwhelming for the child.
- The environment does not create too much or too little stimulation for the child.

Parent responsibilities

- Provide caregiver adequate training for special procedures (e.g., nebulizer, g-tube feeding, finger-prick testing).
- Photocopy written information about the child's special needs for the provider.
- Invite the child care provider to the IEP or IFSP meetings.
- Request consultation with the child care program be written into the IEP or IFSP.
- Plan a method of communication among the family, the child care provider, and any specialists the child sees.

Choosing occasional child care

Everybody needs a break once in a while. No matter how much you love your home and your family, you'll be a more enthusiastic parent if you give yourself time away to recharge yourself. There will be those unexpected times when you'll need to attend to emergencies. In those instances, it is better for children to stay home. Where can you find occasional care?

- **Sitters:** They can be relatives, neighbors, or friends. This care can be at the child's home or outside the home.

- **Exchange care:** Families, neighbors, or friends take turns watching each other's children. If the occasion involves meals and sleepovers, the kids may think the whole time is just for fun.

- **Family child care and center care:** Programs that offer full-time or part-time care may also be available to provide care on an occasional or drop-in basis. Check with these programs to find out about their space availability. Be aware that this type of short-term care may be expensive. Find out how much the charge is before you drop off your child.

No matter how much you love your home and your family, you'll be a more enthusiastic parent if you give yourself time away to recharge yourself.

24

You can find out the quality of the care your child received by the kind of feedback you get from both the caregiver and child. If your son or daughter comes rushing to greet you with "Guess what we did! It was so much fun!" and you see the caregiver beaming, you probably made a good choice.

Whichever care you choose, take these steps:

- **Information:** Leave a card with numbers to call in an emergency and a medical release form for emergency treatment. Explain what you expect your child to do and how to behave while you're gone. Are there chores or homework to be done? What is the bedtime or after-school routine? If the caregiver is younger, give clear instructions about having friends over, what food is allowed, use of the phone and computer, and what television programs your child may watch.

- **Cost:** Determine how much to pay the caregiver or center before you leave. Keep in mind some types of care, such as drop-in care, may be more expensive per hour than other forms of care.

Paying for child care

You have set out to find the best child care possible. You may not be aware, however, just how much of the family budget, and your pay check, will be needed to cover your child care expenses.

In California, care for infants and toddlers costs an average of $550 per month, for a total of $6,500 a year. To find the right provider and keep your budget intact, there are a number of factors and choices you will want to consider.

Your child's age is important because infants and toddlers need more specialized care, and for centers this means more caregivers per child. Centers serving preschoolers require fewer caregivers per child, so the cost can go down as much as $100 to $150 a month.

Where you live may also affect what you pay. Rates in California may vary from county to county and differ from rural to urban areas. Monthly rates also depend on hours of care and whether your child will be receiving extended day, evening, or weekend care.

Also consider additional expenses that can sometimes raise your child care costs substantially. Registration fees, charges for care during special holidays, late pickup fees, and transportation costs can add up quickly. It will also help your budget to ask ahead of time

To find the right provider and keep your budget intact, there are a number of factors and choices you will want to consider.

whether your caregiver allows credits for days when your child is not in care because of illness or vacation.

It's also important to remember that the cost of care does not necessarily equate with its quality. Don't base your assessment of a facility on the fees or on its appearance. You may be surprised to find that a flashy entrance, shiny new equipment, or squeaky-clean everything does not guarantee high-quality child care. So look beyond your first impression and ask yourself: Is this a place where my child will be safe and where the provider will give her the kind of nurturing she needs? Will she learn, be happy, and prosper here? Your child's safety, health, and happiness are, after all, what you are paying for. Child care expenses are an investment and in most instances a necessity. However, selecting the highest quality care pays off many times over in your child's future.

If you find yourself needing help, there are financial resources available in California. Look for subsidized child care programs that may assist you; call 1-800-KIDS-793 for information.

Parent Tip

Depending upon your income, the state may provide assistance in paying for child care. There are several programs which pay the provider on behalf of the family. For more information, call your local child care resource and referral agency.

Licensing

The State of California regulates child care in an effort to protect the health and safety of participating children's personal rights. The California Department of Social Services (CDSS), Community Care Licensing Division (CCL), is responsible for licensing child care centers and family child care homes. The state does not regulate certain types of child care, such as in-home care or persons who care for the children from just one family.

Licensing regulates the number of children to be cared for as well as the number of adult caregivers. Licensing sets staff and caregiver qualifications that are based on education and experience. The caregiver or center must meet specific health, nutrition, maintenance, and safety requirements.

While licensing sets standards for the health and safety of the child care setting, parents should always check out conditions at the child care site for themselves.

The process

Potential applicants for a license must attend an orientation meeting where they receive an application packet and learn about the process. Potential providers must:

- Complete an application.
- Design a written disaster plan.
- Provide fingerprints and complete a child abuse index check.

Family care providers must complete a 15-hour training course that includes pediatric

CPR and first-aid, safety, and health education. Providers are also encouraged to take a variety of classes, such as nutrition and child development.

For child care center programs, at least one person who has finished a 15-hour training course in pediatric CPR and first-aid, safety, and health education must be on site at all times. Center staff must meet certain educational standards; those who care for infants and toddlers must also complete a three-unit course in child development for this age group.

Evaluation

After the provider completes the proper paperwork and training, a licensing analyst makes a general inspection of the care site. The analyst looks at the overall cleanliness and basic childproofing at the facility and insures licensing requirements are met. For family child care homes, such things as swimming pools, fire safety, pets, and any outside major equipment are evaluated during the licensing visit. All electrical outlets accessible to children should have plug protectors. Toxic chemicals and firearms must be locked away or be completely and consistently out of children's reach. Child gates must be installed for areas that are dangerous, such as stairs. While licensing sets standards for the health and safety of the child care setting, parents should always check out conditions at the child care site for themselves.

There are 13 child care licensing offices throughout the state. You can receive your Community Care Licensing office's number by dialing 916-229-4269. These offices also handle most licensing applications. Licensing staff monitor child care facilities through unannounced visits, investigate complaints, revoke licenses if necessary, and work to promote quality child care. Feel free to contact licensing to find out if there are any complaints against a provider and the nature of the complaint. Talk to your provider about any complaints so that you understand her side of the story. Ask to see the licensing reports. In the long run, your instincts, along with your fact gathering, will help you find quality child care.

The first days

You think you have found the right care for your child. You are organized. You are ready to go back to work or start that new job. Then the time comes to drop off your child and suddenly you are filled with mixed emotions. This is normal, understandable, and okay.

Here are some common reactions to the first days at a new child care:

- **Tears:** You and your child may unexpectedly begin to cry. It is normal to feel sad when separating from each other. Know that nearly all parents experience sadness in leaving their child at child care.

- **Stress and anxiety:** Although you may feel confident about your provider, there is always some level of stress regarding the type of care your child will receive. You may wonder about your job or what your first day back will be like. There are many factors that may increase your level of stress for the first few weeks.

- **Joy or relief**: For many parents, going back to work gives welcome relief from day-to-day parenting. Some parents may feel guilty that they feel happy to head into the work force and interact with other adults. Know that in order for your child to be happy, you need to be happy.

You are ready to go back to work or start that new job. Then the time comes to drop off your child and suddenly you are filled with mixed emotions.

8 0 0 - K I D S - 7 9 3

Although you may be sad and anxious regarding the first day, there are benefits for children in child care and for parents who work.

Try these separation strategies:

- Start leaving before you have to go. Prepare. Don't leave it all to the last minute when you are rushed. Let your child bring a favorite toy, blanket, or something special from home.
- Set up a "going out" place in your home close to your front door. Make sure your child's belongings are ready to go the night before.
- When leaving your child at child care, say good-bye clearly and when you know you have your child's attention. Never leave without saying good-bye.
- Leave immediately. Don't hesitate as if something were wrong with your leaving.
- Give your child a reference point for your return that is familiar. Say "I will pick you up after snack time" or refer to another time your child clearly recognizes.
- Always, always return at the time you have given your child for pickup. If you cannot make that time, call and make certain your child is told when you will be there.

Parent Tip

Planning ahead is the secret to avoiding the morning rush hour. Gather toys, clothes, food, and your work items the night before so that you feel prepared for the next day. Check on the current public transportation schedule and what the weather may be like the next day. This helps with some of the early morning unknowns. Keep items, such as the umbrella, sunscreen, diaper bags or backpacks, and a warm hat, together so that you can find these essentials easily in case you need them.

31

Adjusting

Adjustments to care often depend on the age of the child. Each child will vary in the time it takes to adapt to a new caregiving situation. We call this the "trial period." During the first few days, your child needs time to settle into a routine. Don't read too much into how she acts. Your child is learning to separate from you and learning that you will come back. Sometimes the relief of seeing you again can overwhelm your little one. Take your cues from your child as to whether he is ready for a quiet-cuddly hello or a noisy-joyful one.

Knowing what kind of day your child has experienced can relieve your anxiety. If your provider does not already keep written or mental notes on the children in care, you can ask her to do so. The record can be simple—just a few notes on what your child does and learns during the day.

Talking with the caregiver about the transition before care begins may help smooth the process. A gradual separation and entry into child care will ease your child over the adjustment bumps.

Remember that even families that make easy adjustments need to be prepared for separation anxiety to recur. Children often regress after being taken out of care when they are ill or on vacation. Changes at home—a visit from grandma, potty training, a new baby, a divorce, or remarriage—may cause a child to suffer separation anxiety all over again. Changing to a new child care program may also trigger the separation blues. When this happens, look back on your past successes and reassure yourself that they can happen again.

Normal separation milestones

Around seven to nine months of age, and again during the late toddler years, children go through "stranger/separation" anxiety, a common developmental milestone. Many parents mistake the child's normal reaction for evidence of a traumatic event at care. They may feel guilty for subjecting the child to child care. This normal stage usually passes quickly, and children suffer no after effects!

The ride home

It may come as a surprise that one of the most stressful times of the day may be when we pick up our children from child care and take them home. We imagine the moment when we reconnect with our children will be joyful, but at times it's filled with tears, friction, or exhaustion.

Here are some tips to ease your ride home:

- If at all possible, limit the number of hours your child spends at child care. See if you can manage work schedules in which one parent drops the child off as late as possible in the morning and the other parent picks the child up as early as possible. If one parent is unable to help with transportation, perhaps a neighbor or relative could help—even one day a week. Also, keep in mind children tend to be especially tired between 4 and 6 p.m.

- Leave work on time. Take five to ten minutes before quitting time to tie up loose ends and prepare for the next day. Your child will be waiting for you, and leaving work on time will give you more time with her.

- Leave your work at work. When you carry your troubles home, your child will immediately sense your stress. Although your job is important, your children are

We imagine the moment when we reconnect with our children will be joyful, but at times it's filled with tears, friction, or exhaustion.

important too. Remember, your work will be waiting for you tomorrow.

- Hug your child. Tell him how glad you are to see him. Stop and listen, really listen, to him before you go home.

- Tell your child something good about your day. Children are curious about what you do when you are away from them. Tell them a story about your day. The older your child becomes, the more interested she will be in your job.

- Ask about your child's day. Kids experience good and bad days just like adults. Respect your child's feelings and really listen to show you care.

- Keep a snack on hand. It never fails—as soon as you're on the road, your child is hungry or thirsty, starving or dying for a drink of water. He could eat a whole pizza. Having a simple snack, like fruit and cheese, and keeping a water bottle on hand can change the mood of the ride home from grumpy to bright.

- Breast-feed or give your infant a bottle. In the same way a snack makes a difference to an older child, feeding your infant before you get on the road is a wonderful way to reconnect at the end of a busy day.

- Have your child use the bathroom before leaving child care. You want to prevent a scene like this: Your three-year-old is safely strapped into the car seat. You finally make it to the freeway, and yes—you are stuck in traffic. "Dad? I need to go potty. DAAAAD! I really need to go!" In the case of younger children, check with the provider to find out when diapers were last changed.

- Wind down. The trip home can also be a quiet time for both of you. It may be a good time to let your little one catch up on some needed ZZZs.

- Have fun. Listen to music. Sing. End the day with one big solo and you'll have your child laughing, too.

Making your choice work

Once you are happy with your choice, there are some things you can do to help the child care arrangement work out well for everyone. Be sure that you and the caregiver agree upon:

Fees

- Pay on time and make sure you have the funds to cover your check.
- Keep your side of the bargain since you are paying for a service just like any other agreement.

Hours

- Agree on arrival and pickup times.
- Be prompt and respect her hours.
- Be sure you know the overtime policy.
- Remember, your child care provider's job is an important and demanding profession. She often works for 11 or 12 hours a day.
- Know she depends on you to be on time.
- If you are going to be late, call.

Remember, your child care provider's job is an important and demanding profession. She often works for 11 or 12 hours a day. Respect her hours.

Vacations and sick days

- Make sure you notify your provider ahead of time when you will be taking vacation. Find out if there is a vacation credit available.
- Let her know if your child is going to be out of child care for a day or more.
- If you're considering a family child care provider or an in-home provider, find out if there are back-up providers to call when the provider is sick or has a vacation scheduled, and get their names and phone numbers.

Food

- Talk to your provider about nutrition and the meals provided. Does your child have specific requests? Will she be required to eat everything offered?
- What types of meals are provided, and are children included in mealtime setup and preparation?
- Is a menu posted?
- Ask if your provider is receiving a subsidy for children's meals or knows about assistance she can receive from the Child Care Food Program (CCFP). Call 1-800-952-5609 if you would like to learn more about nutrition or to find out how you and your child care provider can participate in the program.

Communication

- Is your provider letting you know about your child's daily activities and progress? Problems? Friendships? Learning styles? Sleeping patterns? When and how will you be notified if your child has a problem?
- Are you letting the provider know about changes that may affect your child in the child care setting?

Your back-up plan

When your child is first enrolled in child care, he will come into contact with other children and—germs! Children have immature immune systems, and it takes time to build up antibodies to all of the germs they will be exposed to. The result may lead to illness causing worries and concerns for parents.

When your child is sick, so are you. What parent has not experienced that helpless, sick-to-the-stomach feeling while cradling a feverish, fussy child? While you need to care for your child, you may also need to work. Parents may find themselves asking: Who will take care of my child? Where? Will my employer understand and be flexible if I stay home with my sick child? Can I use my sick leave or personal days to care for him myself? Is there paperwork I can do from home? Can my partner and I take turns caring for him? Will the child care provider care for her?

Children have immature immune systems, and it takes time to build up antibodies to all of the germs they will be exposed to. The result may lead to illness causing worries and concerns for parents.

The caregiver

"What is your policy regarding illness?" is an important question to ask before enrolling your child in child care. Caregivers should enforce strict sick care policies. As a parent, be sure you understand and are willing to follow these rules—they are for the safety of the caregiver, your child, and all the children at the child care.

37

The caregiver should keep emergency cards near the telephone so parents can be notified quickly in case of illness or accident. Parents should make sure the information on the card is up-to-date. It is the parent's responsibility to be certain that someone—if not the parent, then a relative or friend—is available to pick up your child in case of illness or accident. The caregiver should also notify parents when a child under her care has been diagnosed with a contagious condition.

The parent

Caring for your sick child yourself is the ideal situation for both the parent and child. Yet that is not always possible. Perhaps a grandparent or other family member or trusted neighbor can care for your child. Keep in mind that your child will be healthy most of the time. Make sure you have a back-up plan. By planning ahead and having a child care back-up plan, when she does get sick or the school closes, you will be ready.

Parent Tip

Talk to your employer about the sick-leave policy. Some companies allow employees to take sick leave to care for children, while others only allow sick leave to be used by the employee. If your child or another immediate family member is seriously ill, you may qualify for the Family Medical Leave Act. To learn more about the Family Medical Leave Act, contact the Department of Fair Employment and Housing at 1-800-884-1684.

When concerns arise

Caring for children is important, challenging work. The way a caregiver may approach your child may be different from the way you do. Keep your child's well-being as your number one priority in any conflict resolution. Most important, consider the seriousness of the incident or issue. Use your instincts to decide how to approach the situation. If, at any time, you feel your child is being abused or neglected, immediately remove your child from the caregiver. Report your experience to licensing right away. Do not wait. Do not feel guilty. Your child's safety is the most important thing in the world. Act on your instincts and do not look back.

If you're faced with a situation or incident you don't agree with but which did not harm your child physically or mentally, talk to your provider about it. Stop and think before you discuss this issue with your caregiver. Don't jump to conclusions; make sure you have your facts right and ask questions to clarify any misunderstandings. Talk with your partner, a friend, family member, or child care resource and referral representative about your concern first. If your provider is a friend or family member, be especially sensitive to your personal relationship and try not to be angry when talking to one another.

Keep your child's well-being as your number one priority in any conflict resolution.

39

Here are some tips to help address the problem:
- Talk to your provider. Ask to meet without children present.
- If a face-to-face meeting is not possible, then talk on the telephone.

Parent Tip

There are 13 child care licensing offices throughout the state. Each office also has a child care advocate who can provide information about child care programs and the licensing process. Advocates are a great resource for answering questions and helping you choose quality care. Advocates may also help you if you run into problems with your child care provider.

Call 1-916-229-4269 for more information on how to reach an advocate in your county.

- Explain your concern. Be as specific as you can.
- Refer to the child care policies or contract, if necessary.
- Once you've had your opportunity to speak, then stop and listen to the provider.
- Try to understand her viewpoint. Ask yourself: Was this an isolated incident?

On the other hand, you may find that you and the provider have opposite ways of approaching a situation. The safety and best interest of your child should be your first priority. If, after talking to your provider about your concern, you're not happy with her response, look for child care elsewhere.

Finding new child care

Here are tips for starting your child care search again:
- Make sure you have a clear picture of what you did and did not like about the care of the previous provider.
- Contact your local resource and referral program for help in finding and selecting your next child care provider.
- If possible, establish a trial period before formalizing your caregiver.
- Talk to your child about the transition.
- Trust your instincts.
- Apply what you have learned when you repeat the selection process.

Parental rights

You have the right to check the licensing reports of visits and substantiated complaints of a licensed family child care home or center. Copies of the licensing reports must be kept on-site at family child care homes and centers.
If they are not available on-site, call the California Department of Social Services, Community Care Licensing (CDSS/CCL), at (916) 229-4269 for any inquiries.

As a parent you have the right to ensure your child's well-being while she is in the care of a provider. If you have concerns about the care your child is receiving, trust your instincts. Contact Community Care Licensing and your local resource and referral agency for help and support. Again, if you suspect abuse or neglect, remove your child from the caregiving situation immediately. The information specialist at 1-800-KIDS-793 can provide you with telephone numbers of your local agencies if you are unable to find them.

You have the right to check the licensing reports of visits and substantiated complaints of a licensed family child care home or center. Copies of the licensing reports must be kept on-site at family child care homes and centers. If they are not available on-site, call the California Department of Social Services, Community Care Licensing (CDSS/CCL), at (916) 229-4269 for any inquiries.

You also have the right to report any complaints anonymously about the health and safety of children to CDSS/CCL. In most cases, a visit to the site will take place within 10 days of receiving the complaint. Parents also need to be aware that child care providers are required by law to report any suspected child abuse or neglect.

You make the difference

Get Involved

A successful child care relationship is a two-way process. Tell the provider about your child's needs and listen to the feedback from the provider to be sure she understands and will respond accordingly.

When your child is enrolled in a child care program, one of the greatest gifts you can give him is your personal involvement. Here are some ways to have a positive effect on your child's experience in child care:

- **Become involved:** Your child will spend a big part of her day at child care. Let her know you think it is a special place for her to learn, grow, and have fun. She will get this message best if you show her by making it a part of your own life, not just a spot to drop off and pick up your child.

- **Communicate:** Talking is a two-way process. Tell the provider about your child's needs and listen to the feedback from the provider to be sure she understands and will respond accordingly. Likewise, if the provider tells you about a problem, let her know you understand. Tell her about any changes that may affect your child's behavior, such as moving, a visit from a relative, or a new friend.

- **Discuss concerns:** Many times parents want to talk about a problem right away during pickup time. Your provider may find it stressful to talk when there are still other children in her care. Ask her when a good time would be to discuss the problem, either face-to-face or, if that is not possible, by phone.

- **Volunteer:** If you can volunteer an hour or so during school or child care, you'll not only be a help to the provider, but also get a better picture of your child's experience there. Try a simple activity, such as reading during story time or helping with a planned activity. You'll brighten your child's day, and you'll have a memory to cherish together.

- **Support:** Give support to your child as well as the caregiver by making sure the child is well fed and properly dressed in the morning. If the provider wishes, take an extra set of clothes, a snack, diapers, or any other items she may need. Ask about toy policies and follow them.

- **Advocate:** In order for child care to improve, society needs to understand the importance of quality care. Family involvement is a way to show your support. Be an advocate for quality child care at your work and in your community. Find out about current issues affecting child care. Write letters to the editor of your local paper and to your political leaders asking for their attention to provider training and other compensation issues.

Parent Tip

Did you know there is a law called the Family-School Partnership Act that allows parents to participate in their children's school or child care activities? The law says if you work for a business with 25 or more employees at the same location, you may take off up to 40 hours each year (up to eight hours in any calendar month) to participate in school or child care activities. The law allows you to use vacation, personal leave, or compensatory time for this purpose.

Ages and stages of development

Choosing quality care that is in a healthy and safe environment should be your number one priority. Look for child care that stimulates and encourages your child's physical, intellectual, and social growth. Keep your child's age and personality in mind when looking for the program that best meets his needs. Understanding what makes your child feel secure and knowing the activities he enjoys and will learn from will make a difference in your final child care decision.

Personality

Each child has his own personality and responds to caregivers or experiences differently. Just like adults, children may have outgoing, shy, or even-tempered natures. Your caregiver should be in tune with your child's special personality and treat your child in a positive and caring manner that agrees with his special personality. This is crucial to nurturing his healthy emotional growth. By understanding your child's personality, you and your caregiver can help him succeed by offering care, activities, and discipline that best fit his needs.

As your child grows, you may find yourself searching for clues to her behavior. As a parent, you may hear the words "developmental stages." This is just another way of saying your child is moving through a certain time period in the growing-up process.

Developmental stages

As your child grows, you may find yourself searching for clues to her behavior. As a parent, you may hear the words "developmental stages." This is just another way of saying your child is moving through a certain time period in the growing-up process. At times, she may be fascinated with her hands, her feet, and her mouth. As she grows, she may get into everything. Lock your doors and cabinets, and take a deep breath during those exploration years! Then there will be an age when independence is all she wants. At every stage, what she needs is your love, understanding, and time.

Learning styles

Children learn in many different ways. Each child has his own way of learning—some learn visually, others through touch, taste, and sound. Watch a group of children and you'll understand at once what this means. One child will sit and listen patiently, another cannot wait to move and count beads. Another wants you to show her the answer over and over. Children also learn in different ways depending on their developmental stage. One

Parent Tip

Recent brain research indicates that birth to age three are the most important years in a child's development. Here are some tips to consider during your child's early years:

- Be warm, loving, and responsive.
- Talk, read, and sing to your child.
- Establish routines and rituals.
- Encourage safe exploration and play.
- Make TV watching selective.
- Use discipline as an opportunity to teach.
- Recognize that each child is unique.
- Choose quality child care and stay involved.
- Take care of yourself.

For more information about the first three years, contact the "I Am Your Child" Public Education Campaign at 1-888-447-3400.

thing we know is all children love to learn new things by exploring and discovering. Children love to solve problems during play and in daily activities.

Look for a child care provider who understands children's learning styles and includes reading, learning numbers, art activities, rhyming, and problem solving in your child's daily activities. Also, find out how your provider encourages your child to understand and benefit from daily activities and experiences.

Ages and stages

Depending upon the age of your child, his learning style and personality, your child will have different needs. The first five years are especially crucial for physical, intellectual, and social-emotional development. Keep your child's personality and age in mind when looking for child care experiences and activities. The following pages provide insight into a child's developmental stages from birth through fourteen years.

Birth to eighteen months: an overview

In the first eighteen months after birth, an infant makes miraculous progress. In this relatively short time span, an infant sees her world through her senses. Babies gather information through touch, taste, smell, sight, and sound. To help infants mature and learn, the caregiver should stimulate but not overwhelm them. The overall goal is not to "teach" your baby but to interact and explore her world with her. Older infants are on the move. They take great pleasure in discovering what they can do with their voice, hands, feet, and toes. Soon they practice rolling skills, crawling, walking, and other great physical adventures. Through "the eyes of a child," here is what you might expect during the first eighteen months.

One month

What I'm Like: I can't support my own head and I'm awake about one hour in every ten (though it may seem more).

What I Need: I need milk, a smoke-free environment, a warm place to sleep, hugs and kisses, and to hear your loving voice. It's not too early to sing or read to me. The more you talk and introduce different things to me, the more I learn.

Three months

What I'm Like: My hands and feet fascinate me. I'll laugh and coo at them and you. I'm alert for 15 minutes, maybe longer, at a time. I love to listen to you talk and read to me.

What I Need: Talk to me, feed me, and sing to me. My favorite songs are lullabies. Cuddle me. I need fresh air, a ride in a stroller. Give me things to pull and teethe on.

Tips for looking for a child care provider during the first eighteen months of life. Look for a provider who:

- *Is warm and friendly*
- *Interacts with your infant and has eye contact*
- *Talks to your infant while diapering*
- *Includes your infant in activities, but keeps her safe from older children*
- *Avoids the use of walkers*
- *Has feeding and sleeping practices similar to yours*
- *Allows the infant to eat and sleep whenever she wishes rather than follow a schedule*

Five months

What I'm Like: I may be able to roll over and sit with support. I can hold my own toys. I babble and am alert for two hours at a time. I can eat most baby food. Put toys just out of my reach and I will try to reach them. I like to see what I look like and what I am doing.

What I Need: Make sure I'm safe as I'm learning to crawl. I need happy sounds, and I like to be near you. Dance with me, tickle me, and tell me about the world you see.

Nine months

What I'm Like: I'm busy! I like to explore everything! I crawl, sit, pull on furniture, grasp objects, and understand simple commands. I like to be with other babies and I react to their happiness and sadness.

What I Need: I need locks on cabinets with medicines, household cleaners, or other dangerous things. Put away small sharp objects. I need touches, nutritious food, and educational toys to keep me busy.

Twelve months

What I'm Like: I may be able to pull myself up and sidestep around furniture. I may begin walking. I make lots of sounds and say "Mama" and "Dada." I'm curious about flowers, ants, grass, stones, bugs, and dirt. I like to get messy, 'cause that's how I learn. My fingers want to touch everything. I like to play near others close to my age but not always with them. If I'm walking, please walk at my pace.

What I Need: I need lots of cuddling and encouragement. I need a safe place to move around as I will be getting into anything I can get my hands on. Read to me again and again. Sing our favorite songs. Give me freedom to do most things—until I need help. So please stay near.

Twelve to eighteen months

What I'm Like: I like to eat with a spoon, even if I spill. And I will spill, spill, spill. I will explore everything high and low, so please keep me safe. I may have temper tantrums because I have no other way of expressing my feelings or frustrations. Sometimes I'm fearful and cling to you. I like to have evening routines: music, story, and bath time. I like balls, blocks, pull toys, push toys, take apart toys, put together toys, and cuddles. Sometimes I say "No" and mean it. By eighteen months I can walk well by myself, although I fall a lot.

The Toddler's Creed

If I want it, it's mine. If I give it to you and change my mind later, it's mine. If I can take it away from you, it's mine. If it's mine it will never belong to anybody else, no matter what. If we are building something together, all the pieces are mine. If it looks just like mine, it is mine.

I may jump. I say lots of words, especially the word "mine"—because everything is mine! I like it when we play outside or go to a park. I like being with other children. I try to take off my shoes and socks. I like to build with blocks.

What I Need: Let me touch things. Let me try new things with your help, if I need it. I need firm limits and consistency. Please give me praise. The more you talk with me, the earlier I will tell you how I feel and what I need. I need you to observe me and to understand why I'm upset or mad. I need your understanding and patience. I want a routine. I need you to not mind the mess I sometimes make. I need you to say I'm sorry if you made a mistake. And please read to me over and over again!

Eighteen months through two years: an overview

During the next stage of life, your child is beginning to define himself. Look for child care activities that spur his imagination and vocabulary. During the toddler years, children get into everything, so do your best to keep your child safe from a potential accident. Yet, realize accidents do happen even to the most careful parents and children.

Two years

What I'm Like: I am loving, affectionate, and responsive to others. I feel sorry or sad when others my age are upset. I may even like to please you. I don't need you so close for protection, but please don't go too far away. I may do the exact opposite of what you want. I may be rigid, not willing to wait or give in. I may even be bossy. "Me" is one of my favorite words. I may have fears, especially of sounds, separation, moving household objects, or that big dog.

When looking for quality care for your toddler, consider:

Is the child care setting safe and does it provide small group sizes and adult-to-child ratios?

Are there enough toys and activities so sharing isn't a problem?

Are there a lot of toys for building which can be put together?

Is there a dress-up area?

Do art activities allow the children the freedom to make their own art or do all crafts look the same?

And last, what are the toilet training and discipline practices of the provider?

What I Need: I need to continue exploring the world, down the block, the parks, library, and stores, etc. I like my routines. If you have to change them, do so slowly. I need you to notice what I do well and PRAISE me. Give me two OK choices to distract me when I begin to say "No." I need you to be in control and make decisions when I'm unable to do so. I do better when you plan ahead. Be FIRM with me about the rules, but CALM when I forget or disagree. And please be patient because I am doing my best to please you, even though I may not act that way.

Three through five years: an overview

During the preschool years, your child will be incredibly busy. Cutting, pasting, painting, and singing are all daily activities. When your child starts kindergarten around age five, make sure home and child care activities include learning numbers, letters, and simple directions. Most public school kindergarten programs are usually only a few hours a day. You may need care before and after school. It is never too early to begin your search.

Three years

What I'm Like: Watch out! I am charged
with physical energy. I do things on my
own terms. My mind is a sponge. Reading
and socializing are essential in getting me
ready for school. I like to pretend a lot and
enjoy scribbling on everything. I am full of
questions, many of which are "Why?" I
become fairly reliable about using the
potty. I may stay dry at night and may not.
Playing and trying new things out are how
I learn. Sometimes I like to share. I begin
to listen more and begin to understand
how to solve problems for myself.

What I Need: I want to know about
everything and understand words, and
when encouraged, I will use words instead
of grabbing, crying, or pushing. Play with
me, sing to me, and let's pretend!

Four years

What I'm Like: I'm in an active stage,
running, hopping, jumping, and
climbing. I love to question "Why?" and
"How?" I'm interested in numbers and
the world around me. I enjoy playing
with my friends. I like to be creative with
my drawings, and I may like my pictures
to be different from everyone else's. I'm
curious about "sleepovers" but am not
sure if I'm ready yet. I may want to be
just like my older sister or brother. I am
proud that I am so BIG now!

*When looking for
quality care for your
preschooler, consider:
Are there other children
the same age or close in
age to your child?
Is there space for
climbing, running, and
jumping?
Are there books and
learning activities to
prepare your child for
school?
Is television and movie
watching selective?
Are learning materials
and teaching styles age-
appropriate and
respectful of children's
cultural and ethnic
heritage?
Are caregivers
experienced and
trained in early
childhood development?
Are children given
choices to do and learn
things for themselves?
Are children rushed to
complete activities or
tasks? Or are they
given enough time to
work at their own
pace?*

When looking for quality care for your school-age child, consider:
Is the staff or provider trained to work with school-age children?
Is there space for sports activities, climbing, running, and jumping?
Are there materials that will interest your child?
Is television and movie watching selective?
Is there a quiet place to do homework or read?
Is transportation available?

What I Need: I need to explore, to try out, and to test limits. Giving me room to grow doesn't mean letting me do everything. I need reasonable limits set for my own protection and for others. Let me know clearly what is or isn't to be expected. I need to learn to give and take and play well with others. I need to be read to, talked to, and listened to. I need to be given choices and to learn things in my own way. Label objects and describe what's happening to me so I can learn new words and things.

Five years

What I'm Like: I'm slowing a little in growth. I have good motor control, but my small muscles aren't as developed as my large muscles for jumping. My activity level is high and my play has direction. I like writing my name, drawing pictures, making projects, and going to the library. I'm more interested now in doing group activities, sharing things and my feelings. I like quiet time away from the other kids from time to time. I may be anxious to begin kindergarten.

What I Need: I need the opportunity for plenty of active play. I need to do things for myself. I like to have choices in how I learn new things. But most of all, I need your love and assurance that I'm important. I need time, patience, understanding, and genuine attention. I am learning about who I am and how I fit in with others. I need to know how I am doing in a positive way. I understand more about things and how they work, so you can give me a more detailed answer. I have a big imagination and pretend a lot. Although I'm becoming taller, your lap is still one of my favorite places.

Six through eight years: an overview

Children at this age have busy days filled with recess, homework, and tear-jerking fights with their friends. They begin to think and plan ahead. They have a thousand questions. This age group has good and bad days just like adults. Get ready, because it's only the beginning!

Six years

What I'm Like: Affectionate and excited over school, I go eagerly most of the time. I am self-centered and can be quite demanding. I think of myself as a big kid now. I can be impatient, wanting my demands to be met NOW. Yet I may take forever to do ordinary things. I like to be with older children more than with younger ones. I often have one close friend, and sometimes we will exclude a third child.

What I Need: This might be my first year in real school. Although it's fun, it's also scary. I need you to provide a safe place for me. Routines and consistency are important. Don't accept my behavior

one day and correct me for the same behavior tomorrow. Set up and explain rules about daily routines like playtime and bedtime. I need your praise for what I am doing well. Since I may go to before-and after-school care, help me get organized the night before. Make sure I have everything ready for school.

Seven years

What I'm Like: I am often more quiet and sensitive to others than I was at six. Sometimes I can be mean to others my age and younger. I may hurt their feelings, but I really don't mean to. I tend to be more polite and agreeable to adult suggestions. By now I am conscious of my schoolwork and am beginning to compare my work and myself with others. I want my schoolwork to look "right." If I make mistakes, I can easily become frustrated.

What I Need: I need to tell you about my experiences, and I need the attention of other adult listeners. I really want you to listen to me and understand my feelings. Please don't put me down or tell me I can't do it—help me to learn in a positive way. Please check my homework and reading assignments. Let me go over to my friends and play when possible. I still need hugs, kisses, and a bedtime story.

Eight years

What I'm Like: My curiosity and eagerness to explore new things continues to grow. Friends are more important. I enjoy playing and being with peers. Recess may be my favorite "subject" in school. I may follow you around the house just to find out how you feel and think, especially about me. I am also beginning to be aware of adults as individuals and am curious about what they do at work. Around the house or at child care, I can be quite helpful.

What I Need: My concept of an independent self has been developing. I assert my individuality, and there are bound to be conflicts. I am expected to learn and read and to get along with others. I need support in my efforts so that I will have a desire for achievement. Your expectations will have a big impact on me. If I am not doing well in school, explain to me that everyone learns at a different pace, and that tiny improvements make a difference. Tell me that the most important thing is to do my best. You can ask my teachers for ways to help me at home. Problems in reading and writing should be handled now to avoid more trouble later. And busy eight-year-olds are usually hungry!

Nine through eleven years: an overview

Children from nine to eleven are like the socks they buy, with a great range of stretch. Some are still "little kids" and others are quite mature. Some are already entering puberty, with body, emotions, and attitude changes during this stage. Parents need to take these changes into account when they are choosing child care for this age group. These children begin to think logically and like to work on real tasks, such as mowing lawns or baking. They have a lot of natural curiosity about living things and enjoy having pets.

As children enter adolescence, they want their independence. Yet they still want to be children and need your guidance. As your child grows, it's easier to leave him at home for longer periods of time and also ask him to care for younger children. Trust your instincts and watch your child to make sure you are not placing too much responsibility on him at one time. Talk to him. Keep the door open. Make sure he is comfortable with a new role of caregiver and is still able to finish his school work and other projects.

What I'm Like: I have lots of energy, and physical activities are important to me. I like to take part in sports and group activities. I like clothes, music, and my friends. I'm invited to sleepovers and to friends' houses often. I want my hair cut a certain way. I'm not as sure about school as I am about my social life. Those of us who are girls are often taller and heavier than the boys. Some girls may be beginning to show signs of puberty, and we may be self-conscious about that. I feel powerful and independent, as though I know what to do and how to do it. I can think for myself and want to be independent. I may be eager to become an adult.

What I Need: I need you to keep communication lines open by setting rules and giving reasons for them, by being a good listener, and by planning ahead for changes in the schedule. Remember, I am still a child so don't expect me to act like an adult. Know that I like to be an active member of my household, to help plan activities, and to be a part of the decision-making. Once I am eleven or older, I may be ready to take care of myself from time to time rather than go to child care. I still need adult help and encouragement in doing my homework.

Eleven through fourteen years: an overview

Your child is changing so fast—in body, mind, and emotions—that you hardly know her anymore. One day she's as responsible and cooperative as an adult; the next day she's more like a six-year-old. Planning beyond today's baseball game or slumber party is hard. One minute she's sunny and enthusiastic. The next she's gloomy and silent. Keep cool. These children are in process; they're becoming more self-sufficient. It's Independence Day!

What I'm Like: I'm more independent than I used to be, but I'm quite self-conscious. I think more like an adult, but there's no simple answer. I like to talk about issues in the adult world. I like to think for myself, and though I often feel confused, my opinions are important to me, and I want others to respect them. I seem to be moving away from my family. Friends are more important than ever. To have them like me, I sometimes act in ways that adults disapprove of. But I still need reasonable rules set by adults. However, I'm more understanding and cooperative. I want nothing to do with babysitters—in fact, if I'm mature enough I can often be by myself or watch others.

What I Need: I need to know my family is behind me no matter how I may stumble in my attempts to grow up. This growing up is serious business, and I need to laugh and play a lot to lighten up and keep my balance. I need you to understand that I'm doing my best and to encourage me to see my mistakes as learning experiences. Please don't tease me about my clothes, hair, boy or girl friends. I also need privacy with my own space and things.

Home alone?

If you are just beginning to search for child care, it may seem as though it will be years before you'll be able to leave your child alone. However, time flies, and before you know it, your infant has grown up and is in middle school. There may be a short errand you need to run or a day when your child will arrive home from school 20 minutes before you get home from work. Is it okay to let your child be home alone?

Although there's no sure sign to let you know when your child is ready to be left home alone, the following checklist may help:

- Would your child rather stay home than go to a child care or after-school program?
- Is he easily frightened?
- Is she responsible?
- Can he creatively solve problems?
- Would she spend her time responsibly?
- Does your child become bored easily?
- Does he always let you know where he is going and when he will return?
- Would she be at home with an older brother or sister? Do siblings get along?
- Would the older sibling resent caring for the younger one?
- Would caring for the younger sibling restrict the older child's activities?
- Do you live in an isolated area without close neighbors?

When your child begins to stay at home, let your child know that he may change his mind and go back to after-school care if he chooses.

60

Consider establishing
rules on the
following:

- *How long your
  child will be alone*

- *Which friends may
  come to your home*

- *Television—what
  programs may be
  watched?*

- *Food she may eat*

- *Using the stove,
  telephone,
  computer,
  appliances, or tools*

- *Leaving the house*

- *How she can reach
  you*

- Is your neighborhood safe?
- Will you or another adult always be available to your child in case of an emergency?
- Is a neighbor home to help if needed?

How would your child handle:

- Strangers on the telephone or at the door?
- Being locked out of the house? Fire?
- Arguments with a sister or brother?
- An insect bite or a skinned knee?

Before your child stays home alone, write out the house rules and put them in an easy-to-find place. Let your child know that he may change his mind and go back to after-school care if he chooses. Decide on a trial period to iron out the wrinkles and modify the rules if needed. At this time, you may decide it is best to put your child back into a child care program. Use the trial period to review house rules, first aid, and safety skills.

The balancing act

Congratulations! You now have more child care information than you ever knew existed. The life you are entering into may be overwhelming at times. You're going to be balancing work, household duties, and child care. That's a lot! You'll have times when life runs smoothly, then out of the blue, your child is sick and your car breaks down. That's when you start to scramble. It's easy to get angry and want to quit. It's at these times you need to stop and look at the big picture. Your life may be more rewarding by providing for your children, learning new job skills, and being counted on as a vital part of the work force. At the same time, your children can learn, play, and socialize with others every day at child care.

If you need help, ask your child care provider, ask your friends, ask your co-workers. It's amazing how people are willing to help. But first, you must ask. Although it may be

800-KIDS-793

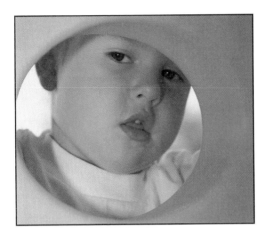

hard to reach out, it is the only way to build a support system and back-up plans that work. The only certainty about being a parent is that nothing is really certain at all. So when you're working, you need child care options, especially if your provider is unavailable or your child is sick. The right support system and back-up plan may make a difference in your success at work and as a parent.

Parenting takes a lot of work. Factor in a job, family life, kids, more kids, schedules, summer vacations, car pools, and bills, plus all the other bumps in the road, and it's amazing what we do manage to accomplish.

After all is said and done—after you've read and listened to all the suggestions of others—trust your own instincts. You know best the right child care arrangement, the one that meets your needs so that you can keep on working, learning, parenting, and smiling.

When you go out into the world, watch out for traffic, hold hands, and stick together.
—Robert Fulghum

You cannot teach a man anything. You can only help him discover it within himself.
—Galileo Galilei (1564-1642)

You give but little when you give of your possessions. It is when you give of yourself that you truly give.
—Kahlil Gibran, The Prophet

The moment you "teach" a child something you have taken away for life her ability to discover it.
—Piaget

63

Child care checklist

☐ The provider/staff is open and welcoming to me and to my child. She/he smiles and looks directly at me and my child.

☐ The caregiver's environment is safe and stimulating.

☐ The caregiver speaks to children in a positive, cheerful tone.

☐ The caregiver seems to enjoy working with children.

☐ I can visit the caregiver/program anytime during hours of operation.

☐ I feel my child will thrive both mentally and physically with this caregiving situation.

☐ The caregiver has training and experience working with children who are my child's age.

☐ Meals provided are age-appropriate, nutritious, and attractive to the child.

☐ My philosophy, values, and discipline techniques closely resemble those of the caregiver.

☐ There is enough space indoors and out so that the children can move about freely.

☐ The program offers activities that my child will enjoy and that are right for his/her age.

☐ Children are encouraged to be creative and to explore new things.

☐ The rooms are comfortable, interesting, and cheerful.

☐ There is adequate lighting, heating, and ventilation.

☐ I can communicate easily and openly with the caregiver.

☐ Information about my child's progress and behavior will be shared with me.

☐ I have been introduced to all the adults who will be providing care for my child.

☐ The caregiver has offered to give me parent references.

800-KIDS-793

❏ I have contacted Community Care Licensing and/or TrustLine to check on the previous history of the caregiver. Call 1-800-KIDS-793 for your local Community Care Licensing or 1-916-229-4269. Trustline may be reached at 1-800-822-8420.

❏ All equipment is safe and in good working condition.

❏ Medicines, poisons, firearms, knives, cleaning chemicals are stored away out of the children's reach. Wall outlets are covered. Stairways have non-pressure safety gates. Window-blind cords are up high, away from any sleeping or play areas.

❏ There is a working fire extinguisher and recently tested smoke alarms.

❏ The caregiver is certified in CPR and first aid.

❏ I understand the policies of the caregiver. There is something in writing that explains the business side of the child care arrangement.

❏ I have a back-up plan in case my child or caregiver is ill or an emergency arises.

❏ I have emergency numbers and a medical release on hand with the caregiver.

❏ I understand all the costs involved with the caregiver. I have asked about extra expenses, such as late fees, supplies, field trips, food, formula, and diapers. I know how much I should pay each month.

❏ I feel comfortable that I can leave my child with this caregiver and that my child will be safe, happy, and loved.

Resources

American Red Cross
1-800-234-5272

Consumer Product Safety Commission
1-800-638-CPSC

California Resource & Referral Network
1-415-882-0234

The Child Care Connection
1-800-KIDS-793

Community Care Licensing, California Dept. of Social Services
1-916-229-4269

Head Start
1-916-323-9727

Nutrition Services Division
1-800-952-5609

San Francisco Child Care Law Center
1-415-495-5498

Special Education, California Dept. of Education
1-916-445-4613

TrustLine
1-800-822-8490

Organizations that contributed to this guide:

- California Child Care Resource and Referral Network, 111 New Montgomery St., 7th Floor, San Francisco, CA 94105, (415) 882-0234.
- Child Action, Inc. 9961 Horn Rd., Sacramento, CA 95827 (916) 369-0191
- Central Valley Children's Services Network, 5030 E. University, Fresno, CA 93727, (559) 456-8195.
- Child Care Health Program, 1322 Webster St., #402, Oakland, CA 94612, (800) 333-3212, (510) 839-1195.
- The Children's Council of San Francisco, One Second St., San Francisco, CA 94105-3407. Administration office, (415) 243-0700, referrals (415) 243-0111.
- Family Resources and Referral Center serving San Joaquin County, (209) 948-1553 or 1-800-526-1555. *The "ages and stages" section of this guide is based on an original special child development brochure designed for the Week of the Young Child by the Community Advisory Committee and Staff.*
- National Association for the Education of Young Children (NAEYC), 1509 16th St., NW, Washington, DC 20036-1426, (202) 232-8777, (800) 424-2460.
- Parent Voices, 111 New Montgomery St., 7th Floor, San Francisco, CA 94105, (415) 882-0234.